COMMUNICATING WITH **CONFIDENCE**™

THE RIGHT WORDS

KNOWING WHAT TO SAY AND HOW TO SAY IT

JENNIFER LANDAU

ROSEN
PUBLISHING®

New York

For Caleb, my favorite communicator

Published in 2012 by The Rosen Publishing Group, Inc.
29 East 21st Street, New York, NY 10010

Copyright © 2012 by The Rosen Publishing Group, Inc.

First Edition

Library of Congress Cataloging-in-Publication Data

Landau, Jennifer, 1961–
The right words: knowing what to say and how to say it/Jennifer Landau.
    p. cm.—(Communicating with confidence)
Includes bibliographical references and index.
ISBN 978-1-4488-5519-3 (library binding)—
ISBN 978-1-4488-5637-4 (pbk.)—
ISBN 978-1-4488-5638-1 (6-pack)
1. Interpersonal communication in adolescence—Juvenile literature.
2. Interpersonal communication—Juvenile literature. I. Title.
BF724.3.I55L36 2012
153.6–dc22

                                                                            2011007019

Manufactured in the United States of America

CPSIA Compliance Information: Batch #W12YA: For further information, contact Rosen Publishing, New York, New York, at 1-800-237-9932.

CONTENTS

4 INTRODUCTION

7 CHAPTER 1
THE RIGHT WORDS TO USE WITH TEACHERS, COACHES, AND COUNSELORS

17 CHAPTER 2
THE RIGHT WORDS TO USE WITH CLASSMATES

30 CHAPTER 3
THE RIGHT WORDS TO USE IN YOUR FAMILY LIFE

41 CHAPTER 4
THE RIGHT WORDS TO USE IN YOUR SOCIAL LIFE

51 CHAPTER 5
THE RIGHT WORDS TO USE ON THE JOB

59 CHAPTER 6
THE RIGHT WORDS TO USE IN ELECTRONIC COMMUNICATION

69 GLOSSARY

71 FOR MORE INFORMATION

74 FOR FURTHER READING

75 BIBLIOGRAPHY

77 INDEX

INTRODUCTION

Have you ever found yourself fumbling for words when trying to talk with someone about an important topic? You tell yourself that it shouldn't be hard to find the right words, yet your sweaty palms and racing heart tell you otherwise. Maybe you need to let your teacher know that the last science exam confused you. Perhaps you want to tell your boss about a problem with a coworker without seeming like you're whining. Since the other person is not a mind reader, your inability to communicate clearly leaves both of you feeling frustrated. You could even end up turning a situation that's no big deal into something more troubling. Who hasn't set out to resolve a conflict only to find that it's gotten worse without anyone being able to pinpoint exactly what went wrong?

Effective communication does take a bit of work. The great news is that there are skills you can learn to become a better communicator. These skills can be applied to a wide range of circumstances: at school or on the job, with family or friends, in person or—with some adjustments—through electronic means as well. When you know how to express yourself clearly, your relationships become far more productive.

Learning how to communicate effectively will have a positive impact on all aspects of your life.

Of course, not everyone you talk with is going to become your lifelong friend or mentor. But when you speak to someone in a way that honors his or her dignity, the interaction will go a lot more smoothly. The adage "Sticks and stones can break my bones, but words will never hurt me" just isn't true. Words can cause tremendous damage, especially in the digital age when a cruel comment seems to spread faster than the speed of light. Scan the news or speak to someone who's been the victim of verbal bullying and you soon realize how vital it is to choose your words with care.

Throughout this book, there are tips and strategies to teach you to speak with confidence in many different settings. You'll learn the importance of timing your conversations well so that you don't approach another person when he or she is least inclined to hear you out. You'll learn to watch your tone: the *way* you say things so that you don't come across as angrier (or more anxious or puzzled) than you really are. In addition, you'll find out how listening attentively to someone else's point of view can turn you into an expert communicator. Taken together, these skills will help you reach your goals in life and feel happier and more in control in the process.

THE RIGHT WORDS TO USE WITH TEACHERS, COACHES, AND COUNSELORS

Whether a school is in a rural, suburban, or urban environment, students have to interact with a variety of adults within their school day. Teachers, guidance counselors, and coaches are just some of the school personnel they will encounter on a daily basis. Learning the skills to communicate effectively with these various adults—learning not just *what* to say but *how* best to say it—will go a long way toward making the school experience a positive one.

It takes a bit of practice to figure out the right approach for each situation. In most cases, it's important to have a goal in mind when preparing to address an adult at school. People don't get in their cars and wander around aimlessly hoping to reach their destination. If they are not sure how to get where they're going, they map out a route or set their Global Positioning System (GPS) device, knowing they may have to adjust should circumstances change. Having a goal for the discussion is like setting your conversational GPS. This level of focus will help keep your language clear and concise, a must for any successful interaction.

Talking with Teachers

Whatever a teacher's personal style (some are more laid-back by nature, some more standoffish), it is important to remember that he or she is a professional and should be treated with respect. If you have a question for a teacher or a concern you need to address, schedule a meeting at a time that works for both of you. Students are more likely to get their teachers' full attention in this situation, rather than trying to catch them on the way back from lunch or on the way to their car after school.

If you are having a problem keeping up with your schoolwork, let your teacher know as soon as possible. Remember to be specific about your concerns.

Any difficulties with assignments should be addressed as soon as possible. Most students—and their parents—can access their homework and grades online, so claiming to be blindsided at the end of the term is not the right approach. Teachers want to help their students achieve but need to know their specific concerns.

Be clear about the problems you are having in class. Never belittle the teacher when discussing why you're having issues with a particular subject. Saying "Your history lessons are so boring, I tune out" is much less effective than saying "I get confused when you go into detail about the different battles of World War II."

When your teacher explains a concept to you, write it down, and then repeat it back to make sure you understood what was said. It's a good idea to do a few practice math problems or write the introduction to that essay while you are meeting with the teacher.

Singled Out

There may be times when you feel as if your teacher is singling you out for criticism. If this is the case, try not to get defensive, even if emotions are running high. A great way to do this is to use I-messages, which are statements that begin with the word *I*.

I-messages explain how the speaker feels, rather than accusing the other person. With I-messages, you can say what has led you to feel a particular way and what you need from the other person.

Body Language

Communication involves more than verbal or written language. Body language—the movements, gestures, and facial expressions used to convey meaning—is also important. If someone offers an apology while rolling his eyes, he is bound to come across as insincere. Likewise, people who slouch and avoid eye contact may be seen as lacking confidence.

If you are unsure what your body language says about you, take a look in the mirror. Do you stand with your shoulders hunched? Is your expression more pained than peaceful? If so, work on keeping your shoulders square and your facial muscles relaxed. Showing confidence through your body language will help you stay calm and focused on your goal.

Knowing how to read another person's body language will help you figure out how your message is being received. A teacher who keeps backing away as you speak may be feeling like his or her personal space is being invaded. Hit the pause button on your interaction and take a step back to regroup. In a case where the other person seems puzzled or angry based on his or her facial expressions, a different approach may be in order. Paying attention to these nonverbal cues will help you become a more effective communicator.

The goal is for greater understanding between two people, not for one of them to "win" the discussion. Imagine walking into a meeting with a teacher and saying "You pick on me so much in class, you must hate me." Then imagine saying "I feel really embarrassed when you make fun of my handwriting when I come up to the board. Please don't say things like that in front of the whole class." Which comment is more likely to draw a positive response from the teacher?

Coaching Concerns

Coaches can be great mentors to their players. They are there to help their players succeed and should be given the same consideration as teachers and other school personnel. In fact, many coaches have a full teaching load along with their coaching duties.

Should you need to talk with a coach, schedule a meeting as you would with a teacher. If, for example, you are confused about a specific play, don't yell your question across the field. This shows disrespect for both the coach and your teammates. You will come across as immature and impulsive, rather than as someone who is sportsmanlike.

Any concerns about the coach's playing favorites or being unfairly critical should be addressed using I-messages. Saying "You act like Matt is the only player on the team who matters" will only make the coach feel attacked. A comment such as "I feel frustrated that I'm not getting more playing time and wish you would give me a chance to prove myself" will make the coach more likely to hear you out.

If you don't make the team in the first place, ask to meet with the coach to discuss how you can improve your chances for the following season. Both tone of voice and body language count in this situation. Whining, scowling, or standing

Coaches are eager to see their players succeed. Listen carefully to any advice your coach has to offer.

with your arms crossed in front of your chest will not make a good impression. A positive approach, however, shows both determination and team spirit.

There may come a point when you need to quit a sports team for whatever reason. It's far better to be honest with the coach about this decision, rather than to just stop showing up for practice. It's fair to give a brief explanation, but there's no need to go into great detail. Keep it short and focus on how rewarding the experience has been and how much you have grown by being part of the team. Don't forget to mention how sorry you are for having to leave the team at this time.

Getting Guidance

Guidance counselors know the issues that teens face. Whether the problem is stress or peer pressure or trouble at home, guidance counselors have the expertise to help. Meeting with a guidance counselor is one instance where it's OK to be unclear about what you want to say. He or she will work with you as you sort through your feelings.

It's important to be honest and direct when talking with a guidance counselor. This is a situation where you should feel comfortable letting your guard down and speaking from the heart. If you are worried about a college application or anxious because your father lost his job, say so. Trust that the guidance counselor will be sympathetic to your concerns.

If issues with teachers or classmates come up, guidance counselors can help students view the situation from various

Talking with a guidance counselor is a great way to sort through any feelings that come up when dealing with a problem.

angles to figure out the right plan of action. They may even act as a mediator to help resolve a conflict with another person. The guidance counselor's ability to remain objective will help everyone focus on finding a solution, rather than getting stuck in an endless round of finger pointing.

Listening to Suggestions

When a guidance counselor offers suggestions, you should listen without interrupting. You can't know if the advice is of use unless you are willing to hear the details. Focus on what your counselor is saying, rather than what you plan to say next. While it's natural to want to get your point across, you can't be an effective communicator if you don't listen with attention and respect. After the person is finished speaking, repeat back what you heard to make sure you understood.

There may be times when you are so upset that you simply need to vent your feelings. If you are too angry or anxious to listen to your guidance counselor at that moment, schedule a follow-up meeting. Having a safe place to express your emotions is crucial, but at some point a plan of action must be set in place.

It's normal to be worried that news of your problems will get back to classmates or teachers. Tell your guidance counselor about these concerns, but know that most schools have confidentiality agreements in place. Of course, if your counselor becomes aware of a potentially dangerous situation, he or she will have to take action. The safety of students and staff must remain the top priority.

THE RIGHT WORDS TO USE WITH CLASSMATES

Success at school depends on getting along with classmates as well as adults. Some of these classmates will remain lifelong friends. Others will just make great lab partners or study buddies. There will be those, however, who seem intent on causing you or your classmates grief. These are the students who tease or bully their way through the school day. Although it's not possible to have close relationships with everyone, having the right communication skills in your toolkit will help you prepare for many different situations.

In *The Teen's Guide to World Domination*, author Josh Shipp talks about the concept of

Always treat your classmates with compassion. Do your best to build them up by staying positive and offering a helping hand.

"word math." This concept has nothing to do with calculus and everything to do with interacting with others. According to Shipp, anything you say is either going to *add* to someone (build him or her up) or *subtract* from that person (tear him or her down).

It is especially important to keep Shipp's idea in mind when dealing with peers. They are likely facing many of the same issues you are and should be treated with compassion. Always aim to build up the other person with both your verbal and non-verbal communication. There is no downside to staying focused on the positive. That does not mean ignoring problems when they come up at school. The goal is to work toward a solution that shows respect for your classmates and the entire school community.

Schoolwork Struggles

There may be times when a classmate tries to copy off your paper during class. If this happens, start by covering your paper or moving your body so that the other person can't peek. Do this subtly, not by clearing your throat loudly or groaning as you move. The point is to send a message without causing any embarrassment.

Should this behavior continue, take the person aside and state directly that you don't allow anyone to copy your work. If he or she denies doing this, back off and see if it happens again. Your warning may just do the trick. If you have to approach the teacher with your concerns, a general statement such as "I think that some people in the class are trying to cheat" will highlight the issue without singling anyone out.

Working on a project with a classmate who doesn't do his or her fair share can be another frustrating experience. At the outset, divide the work evenly and make sure you keep a record of who is responsible for what tasks. That way when deadlines are missed or parts of the project are left unfinished, it's obvious what has gone wrong.

Keep your cool if your classmates tease you once or twice about something minor. If they see that the teasing doesn't affect you, they will back down.

When approaching a classmate who has fallen behind, don't belittle him or her. The student may be confused or overwhelmed and too embarrassed to approach you. If he or she is simply slacking off, refer back to that list of tasks the two of you developed. Remember to stick to the facts and don't raise your voice or use a sarcastic tone. If you have to bring the teacher into the discussion, stay calm and focused on the project at hand and not your clashing personalities.

Teasing

Teasing is not the same thing as bullying. If a classmate makes a couple of jokes about your recent haircut and then lets it go, that's teasing. Bullying involves a pattern of aggressive behavior that can inflict both emotional and physical harm. Most school districts have a code of conduct in place that is meant to promote mutual respect for all students. Teasing does go on, however, often out of sight of teachers and administrators. While mild teasing can be annoying, try not to lose your cool. If someone says, "Nice

Managing Angry Feelings

It's normal to feel angry when someone says or does something that upsets you. But it's important to learn how to deal with negative emotions. You can't communicate well if your heart is pounding or your stomach is tied up in knots. These kinds of physical reactions will show up in your body language, too, making it hard to appear confident. Here are some tips to help you keep it together when those angry feelings strike:

1. In *The Kid's Guide to Working Out Conflicts*, author Naomi Drew suggests that you say the word "stop" to yourself and picture a stop sign whenever you're tempted to strike back at someone. This will remind you to slow down and take control of your emotions.

2. Take a few deep, cleansing breaths. This works wonders for calming your body. Since your body and mind work together to process emotions, taking charge in this way helps you stay focused on what you need to communicate.

3. Drew recommends having calming statements in mind that you can call up when you feel overwhelmed. Sentences such as "I can deal with this," or "I am in charge of my feelings," will remind you to stay upbeat even when someone is pushing your buttons. It may not feel natural to say these things to yourself at first, but over time these statements will help keep you on an even keel.

shirt" in a mocking tone or teases you about a crush, it's best to ignore it or make a joke yourself. Say, "Yeah, that's what you get for buying shirts off the sales rack," and keep on walking. When your classmate sees that you're not crushed by some comment, he or she will likely back down.

Teasing can be about something positive as well, like getting the lead in the school musical. Perhaps the person doing the teasing envies your success or the courage it took to try out in the first place. Whatever the reason, don't apologize for your good fortune. Of course, don't roam the halls singing every song at the top of your lungs, either. If you sense that your classmate might like to be involved in the theater program, encourage him or her to audition next time around. It's a kind gesture and will take the focus off of you, too.

If the teasing really bothers you, don't forget to use I-messages. "I don't think that's funny, so please stop," is a great way to respond. It's a short, direct statement that doesn't provoke the other person. Should the teasing turn into something more threatening, seek help from a trusted adult like a teacher, guidance counselor, or relative.

Fending Off a Bully

Pick up any paper or turn on the TV and it's clear that bullying has reached epidemic proportions. Although school districts have anti-bullying policies in place, teens are still targeted in schools throughout the country. According to the U.S. Health Resources and Services Administration, between 15 to 25 percent of U.S. students are bullied "with some frequency." Physical

If a bully attacks you verbally, use statements such as "It's not OK to talk to me that way" to show that this behavior is unacceptable.

bullying includes things like shoving, tripping, or hitting another student. Psychological bullying can range from giving someone the silent treatment to constantly gossiping about things like his or her weight, style of dress, or sexual orientation. Another

big threat is cyberbullying, which will be discussed in chapter 6.

If a bully verbally assaults you, be clear and direct, and focus on his or her behavior. Make statements such as "It's not OK to talk to me that way" or "What you're saying isn't true, so cut it out." A firm, even tone of voice and steady eye contact will project confidence. You may not feel that way, but act-ing as if you do will help you communicate from a position of strength. If the bully continues lashing out, walk away. You never want to get involved in a drawn-out confrontation.

Physical threats should be taken seriously. Try not to be alone at school and talk to an adult adviser as soon as possible. Although you may feel embarrassed by all this negative attention, remember that you have done nothing wrong. If a bully threatens to harm you if you dare "tattle," let that be known as well. While your instinct might be to shield your parents from your hassles at school, they also need to be involved when your physical well-being is on the line.

Be a Force for Good

Even students who are not the targets of bullies should challenge their bad behavior. Most bullies expect bystanders to look the other way. But if you and your classmates band together, you can help change the culture of your school.

A great place to start is by giving support to the person being bullied. Make it clear that you don't agree with the bully's words or actions. You could offer to walk your classmate to the cafeteria if he or she is feeling anxious, or a group of you could spend time together after school. The more students who get involved, the

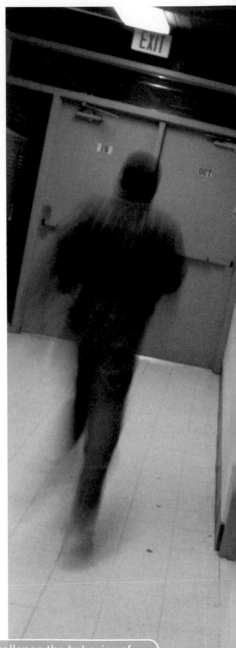

You and your classmates can band together to challenge the behavior of those who treat others with disrespect. Make your school a bully-free zone!

better the outcome. Such solidarity shows the bully that the majority of students want their school environment to be safe and productive.

If you feel comfortable talking with a bully directly, keep your voice calm and even. Don't go into a long discussion or try to be confrontational. A comment such as "Please stop being so mean to Amy. I'm sure you wouldn't want to be treated that way" is enough. If you can, have your fellow classmates do the same. The idea is not to gang up on the bully, but to let him or her know that others disapprove of the bullying. If there is no reasonable way to approach the person, enlist the help of a school counselor or administrator.

MYTHS
and
facts

Myth: If you avoid talking about a problem, it will go away.

Fact: If a problem is troubling enough to cause conflict in a relationship, it can only be resolved through open and honest discussion. Although you might need a cooling-off period after a heated exchange, at some point you have to talk with the other person to try to come up with a solution that meets both of your needs.

Myth: You don't need to work on communicating well. Everyone learns how to talk as children, after all.

Fact: There is a world of difference between "talking" and truly communicating. Effective communication involves a wide range of skills that can only be developed through practice and a commitment to expressing oneself with both clarity and compassion.

Myth: Women are better communicators than men.

Fact: Women and men may communicate differently, but it's unfair to say that women are better at it. In general, men tend to focus on fixing a problem whereas women are more concerned with interpersonal relationships. But you can't resolve issues if you don't have a goal any more than you can ride roughshod over someone's feelings just to get the job done. As with many things, men and women have much to learn from each other in this area.

CHAPTER 3

THE RIGHT WORDS TO USE IN YOUR FAMILY LIFE

It's natural for teenagers to want to be independent and spend more time with friends than with family. That doesn't mean you should treat your parents and siblings like the enemy, though. These are the people who know you best and want you to succeed in all things. They will offer unconditional love and support as you grow toward adulthood.

As long as you are all living under one roof, it makes sense to try to get along. Developing good communication skills will help maintain family harmony. The skills you learn in a family setting can be carried over to other situations that you'll face in your work and personal life.

While every family has issues, learning how to solve problems and resolve conflicts will help keep your family strong. You need to learn how to both talk and listen with care. Being able to understand the perspective of your parents or siblings is also important. When you can put yourself in someone else's shoes, you can avoid a lot of misunderstandings and hurt feelings.

Staying Connected

It is easy to take your family for granted because you don't have to go out of your way to see them on a regular basis. Yet if you don't keep the lines of communication open, it will be that much harder to talk should a problem develop. Don't fall into that trap. Instead, take the time to tell your father that you hope his big meeting goes well. Try saying, "Pass the cereal, please" to your brother or sister, rather than grunting and pointing toward the box. Talk about that funny commercial you saw on television or something interesting that happened at school. Keep those conversational muscles working.

At times it might seem as if parents don't want their kids to have any fun. All they care about are grades and curfews and keeping you away from your friends. If you can see things from their side, however, you will realize that they are concerned about your future. They want you to achieve great things and feel responsible for your well-being. By talking about everyday events with your mom or dad, you strengthen the bond between you. This may help when it comes time to discuss extending a curfew or letting go of some of those high expectations.

Taking the time to share meals and conversation helps families stay close.

Siblings have their own concerns, too. Maybe your little brother is anxious about trying out for the soccer team or your older sister is worried about keeping her part-time job. It's important to remember that everyone has pressures and his or

her own way of dealing with them. Why not let your siblings know that you care by spending time with them and asking about their lives? Kick around a soccer ball with your brother and remind your sister that you are always there should she need to talk. The payoff in terms of closeness and improved communication could be huge.

Talking It Through with Parents

When you need to approach a parent, stepparent, or guardian about an issue, plan ahead. Think about your goal for the conversation. Do you need practical advice? A safe place to vent? Their names on a permission slip? Having a sense of what you need ahead of time will help focus the discussion.

Knowing when to approach someone is vital, too. It's not a good idea to ask Dad for a raise in your allowance when he's fretting over a stack of bills. Don't ask Mom to have a heart-to-heart about a conflict with a friend while she's rushing out the door to work. It's best to get them

If you think carefully about what you want to say before talking with a parent, the discussion will stay focused and productive.

when they are calm and can focus, like during mealtimes or when you're out walking the dog. Say, "I need to talk to you about something. Do you have time for this now?" Showing that level of respect will start the conversation off on the right foot.

When you speak, don't rush. You may have been obsessing about the concert you want to attend for weeks, but this is the first your parents are hearing about it. They need time to process the information and come up with a response. Watch your tone of voice and body language, too. If you come across as relaxed and reasonable, they are going to react in a more positive way.

Of course, don't just appear reasonable, *be* reasonable. If you've kept the lines of communication open, you know how a parent might react to whatever topic you want to discuss. There may be a dance coming up that would cause you to miss your curfew. Asking to stay out an extra half hour makes sense. Demanding to come home three hours late is no way to gain your parents' trust or ease their anxiety.

Family Meetings

The idea of holding a family meeting might seem corny at first. Yet holding a regularly scheduled meeting is a great way to stay in touch and deal with any concerns before they spin out of control. As with all communication, the aim should be problem solving, rather than the laying on of blame.

Set topics for the meeting ahead of time so that everyone knows what's going to be covered. Post the list of topics on the fridge or bulletin board so that all members of the

Holding regular family meetings will help you find solutions to conflicts before they become overwhelming.

family can see it. Once you've gathered, pick one person to take notes and another to make sure the meeting stays on track. When talking about a problem, be as objective as possible. Criticizing a loved one will only lead to greater conflict. Steer clear of name-calling, too. Labeling someone as selfish

or stupid will make that person either lash out or shut down completely.

A comment such as "Molly takes so long in the bathroom that I'm always late for school," is not helpful. Instead ask "How can we make our mornings run more smoothly so we all get to school or work on time?" It may take practice to change your way of speaking to family members. You may be so comfortable with each other that snide comments and name-calling become second nature. But working to fix those bad habits can have a tremendous impact on how you all get along.

As a family, think of several possible solutions to a problem. Pick one to try, and then discuss how it's working at the next scheduled meeting. If, for example, posting a morning bathroom schedule does nothing to get the family out of the house earlier, agree to try something else. These follow-up steps are crucial. You want everyone to feel as if these meetings will bring about needed change in the family dynamic.

The Art of Apologizing

Along with "I'm listening," "I'm sorry" are two of the most powerful words in the English language. The truth is, everyone slips up sometimes. It could be spilling soda all over the couch, borrowing a piece of clothing without asking, or calling your sibling a nasty name. Whatever the case, an apology is in order.

Be honest about what you did wrong, but don't go on about what an awful person you are. It's best to stick to the specifics of the situation and figure out how to prevent the same thing from happening in the future. Your tone of voice and body language make a big difference when apologizing. Spitting out "Hey, I said it was my fault, OK?" while shrugging your shoulders or curling your upper lip does not send the correct message. You'll come across as insincere, which will only cause the hard feelings to continue.

Don't make excuses or bring up the four times that your brother or sister swore at you. No matter how embarrassed or uncomfortable you feel, look the other person in the eye and own up to the mistake. No doubt the time will come when you'll be the one who's owed an apology. Why not set an example of how to do this with grace and goodwill?

Sibling Stress

Siblings share a house and may even share a room. The level of closeness makes it doubly important that you communicate effectively. It may seem hard to appreciate that pesky younger brother or grumpy older sister at times. Yet siblings can be a great source of comfort and support both now and in years to come. Why not put in the effort to make your relationship as constructive as possible?

Never yell at siblings, no matter how angry they've made you feel. Work to understand their point of view and be clear about yours. Maybe your kid brother thought it was no big deal to "borrow" your camera without asking. Instead of saying, "How could you be such an idiot?" say, "I feel like I can't trust you when you take things out of my desk. You need to ask me first." If you're not in attack mode, he'll be much more likely to hear the message and change his way of doing things.

Think of your siblings as a great, untapped resource. That grumpy older sister could be dealing with issues that you will face soon enough. If you've worked to keep the lines of communication open, she will have a lot to teach you. That doesn't mean you should pester her to spill her guts. But when she does talk, pay close attention to her words without judging them or thinking about what you'll say next. Then when it's your turn to talk about a problem you're having, she might just do the same for you.

10 Great Questions

TO ASK A GUIDANCE COUNSELOR

1. How can I tell my teacher that I don't think it's fair that he punishes the whole class when only one of us does something wrong?

2. My coach keeps blaming a teammate for every loss. What can I say to get the coach to stop without taking the heat myself?

3. If I want to take a year off before heading to college, how can I let my parents know without getting them angry?

4. My parents are getting divorced and are saying mean things about each other. Is there a way to talk to them about this without choosing sides?

5. What can I say to my kid brother to get him to give me some space without hurting his feelings?

6. My classmate invited me to a party, but I don't want to go. How can I say no without being mean?

7. I want to join a club, but I'm nervous. How can I break the ice with this new group of people?

8. My boss sometimes uses racially insensitive language. How do I approach her about this without risking my job?

9. People I barely know want to friend me on a social networking site. Should I just ignore them?

10. My friend posted a picture of us together that makes me uncomfortable. What's the best way to ask him to take it down?

THE RIGHT WORDS TO USE IN YOUR SOCIAL LIFE

For many teenagers, friendships and romantic relationships are at the center of their lives. These relationships help them figure out the type of people they want to be and the type of behavior they expect from others. Through their social circle, they are exposed to new interests and different points of view.

It takes practice and patience to learn to communicate well with your peers. Getting your needs met without hurting someone else's feelings can be a tricky proposition. You may have been friends with some of these people for years. Others are new in your life but mean just as much to you. All of you are changing as you grow and mature. Add in the

The best way to maintain a friendship is to keep the lines of communication open.

stress of schoolwork and family life, and it's easy to feel overwhelmed. That's why it's vital to know what matters most to you and how to express those values to those around you.

The Friendship Factor

True friendship is based on trust, respect, and open communication. There can be friction in even the closest friendships, but what matters is how you handle any conflicts that come between you. When you put your energy into expressing yourself clearly and listening without judging, the odds of maintaining the relationship are far greater.

If your friend is dating someone new and seems to have forgotten about you, set aside a time to talk. Start by letting your friend know that you're glad he or she has found someone wonderful. Then you can say that you miss hanging out together like you always did. Never put your friend—or the person he or she is dating—down because *you* feel left out. Hurtful comments will make your friend feel attacked and end any chance at productive communication. Once you've spoken, listen to what he or she says with an open mind. Remember that your goal is to fix the friendship, not to win an argument.

You could be faced with the other extreme: a friend who wants *all* of your time. He or she texts and calls constantly, expecting you to be available twenty-four hours a day. Although the attention might seem flattering at first, it soon becomes a burden. Say something like "Your friendship means a lot to me, but I need time alone and with other friends, too. I can't always get right back to you."

No matter the situation, sensitivity and kindness go a long way. At this age, most friendships last a lot longer than romantic relationships, so don't give up on your friend after one fight. If the two of you speak and nothing gets resolved, give yourselves some time to cool off. Talk things through with an adult you trust, like a relative or guidance counselor. He or she can help you gain perspective and remind you to focus on the positive aspects of the friendship. When you speak with your friend again, you'll be more relaxed and ready to make things right.

Dating Dynamics

Whether you're first asking someone out or trying to handle a problem in your romantic relationship, communication is key. If you care deeply about another person, no subject should be out of bounds. But knowing how and when to say something can make all the difference.

Be clear about your expectations when you begin dating someone. If the two of you are not on the same page, it can lead to trouble later on.

It's nerve-wracking to ask somebody out on a date. Even if you've known this person for a while and hung out in a group, taking that next step can be scary. Acknowledge that fact and use it to help you prepare. Work on projecting confidence through your body language and tone of voice. Use deep breathing techniques to help you stay in control.

If you are asking him or her out in person, make sure you're alone so that you don't have to worry about other people's reactions. A simple "Would you like to see a movie this week-end?" works fine. Should the answer be "no," thank him or her for hearing you out, and leave it at that. Trying to convince someone to go out with you is a drain on both your energy and self-esteem.

Once you start dating, make sure you keep talking. That doesn't mean you have to tell the other person every thought that crosses your mind. It does mean dealing with any problems that crop up, rather than letting bad feelings take root. Be clear about your expectations, too. If one of you wants to date casually and the other wants more of a commitment, you need to find a compromise that works for both of you. You have to be honest—with yourself and with the person you're dating—if you want a relationship that can go the distance.

It could be that your boyfriend or girlfriend treats you with kindness and respect when the two of you are alone. Get him or her around friends, however, and you feel like you're either being insulted or ignored. When you talk about this, be sure to use an I-statement such as "I feel rejected when you tease me or act like I don't exist. I need you to be nice to me when we're with your friends."

Ending a Friendship or Romance

At some point, you may need to end a friendship or romantic relationship. Maybe your friend is spending time with people who make you uncomfortable and shuts you out whenever you bring up the subject. It could be that your boyfriend or girlfriend has betrayed your trust by seeing someone else behind your back.

If you have to end things, do it in person. Never send a text or e-mail or change your Facebook status to get your message across. Such actions are not only cruel but also short-sighted because you're bound to run into your ex again. Find a quiet place to talk, and be certain about what you want to say before you meet. That way you'll stick to your guns if he or she tries to change your mind.

Keep the conversation short. If you've known your friend since second grade, don't bring up every unkind word that's passed between you since then. Zone in on what is happening now and why you need to say good-bye. If it's a romance that's ending, be clear that it is over for good. You may think you're being nice by leaving the door open for another try, but this will only make things more painful for both of you.

Expect to feel sad when any type of relationship ends. But stay open to making new friends as well. Talk to the girl who made that interesting comment in English class. Invite the shy A-student to work on a school project together. The more you stay focused on the future, the easier it will be to heal the wounds of the past.

Whatever the situation, your truthfulness should trigger the same response in the person you're dating. If he or she refuses to talk, don't force a conversation at that moment, but don't deny your own feelings. Ask to talk about what's bugging you a little while later. A pattern of your boyfriend or girlfriend clamming up is a bad sign. No relationship can survive for long without a free flow of communication.

Peer Pressure

Everyone has a need to belong and to feel accepted. The pressure to go along with the crowd is especially strong in the teenage years. This type of peer pressure can make it difficult to know what to think and how to act. Here's where good listening skills come into play. This involves listening not only to what your friends are saying but to your inner voice as well. Whether you call that your conscience or your gut, it's what tells you if your words and actions line up with your beliefs. When you're certain of what you believe, it's much easier to communicate those feelings to others.

Suppose your friends think it's OK to skip school occasionally. Maybe they exclude people from your group because of the clothes they wear or because they're not jocks. If you think this is wrong, say so. Statements like "I think it's important to be in school every day I can," or "I don't see why Sean can't sit with us just because he doesn't play football" will let your friends know your opinion.

Speak your mind if you feel like you're being pressured into doing something you know is wrong. True friends will respect your point of view.

Peer pressure can be especially strong in social situations like parties. Sometimes understatement works best in these circumstances. If people are drinking or smoking and expect you to do the same, a simple "No thanks" or "I'll pass" should suffice. You can always "blame" your parents, too. Say, "Oh, my parents would ground me for a year if I came home stinking of cigarettes."

It's not easy to speak out like this. Others may make fun of you or refuse to talk to you altogether. You may even find that you're no longer invited to certain parties or other social events. But the truth is, friends who act like this are not really your friends. It's OK to work to repair those relationships if you believe they can be improved. Yet in the long run, staying true to who you are and feeling free to speak your mind will lead to a much happier life.

THE RIGHT WORDS TO USE ON THE JOB

At one time or another, most people will have to find employment. Whether it's a part-time job after school or a full-time job after college, there are specific communication skills you need to use at work. You will have to deal with a variety of people on the job: bosses, coworkers, and in some cases, customers. Knowing the right words to use when faced with different situations will make you an invaluable member of any team.

Throughout the course of this book, you've learned that effective communication requires a clear goal. Of course, your first goal in the world of work is to be hired. That usually means being interviewed by one or more people. Interviews can be intimidating experiences, especially when you are new to the process. But there are steps you can take to make sure you present your best self when speaking with potential employers.

The Interview Process

Even a part-time or summer job could lead to a life-changing experience, so take every opportunity seriously. Prepare for the interview by researching the company and coming up with some set answers to common questions. You don't want to look like you're following a script, but you don't want to be caught off guard by basic questions, either. When you put in the effort to research the company you're interviewing with, you come across as knowledgeable and enthusiastic. Take care to dress professionally, too. The way you present yourself speaks volumes to a potential employer.

Watch your body language as soon as you enter the work-place. When the interviewer greets you, look him or her in the eye, shake hands, and stand up straight to project confidence. Once you're seated, don't slump in your chair or stare off to the side, either. The way you carry yourself throughout the meeting will make a big impression on the interviewer. Make sure it's a positive one.

When you two begin talking, pay close attention to what the interviewer is saying. Give concise answers to any questions you're asked. Your goal is to show how your talents will enhance the company where you're hoping to work. It's a good idea to ask questions, too, as this underscores your interest in the position. Show curiosity about that new product they're developing or mention some other tidbit you've gathered from your research. Don't begin the interview by asking about benefits or employee discounts. Although those questions are legitimate, if you lead with them, you'll come across as focused on your needs, rather than the needs of the company.

If you project a positive image through your words and body language, your job interview will go more smoothly.

After the interview, don't forget to send a follow-up letter or e-mail. Thank the interviewer for the opportunity and reiterate why your background makes you the right candidate for the job. Check for typos and watch your tone. This is a professional exchange, not a text to your best buddy.

Off to a Good Start

Work hard to create a great first impression when you start a job. Be polite to everyone you meet and attentive when your boss and coworkers speak to you. If you have questions, make sure they are relevant to the position and provide information you couldn't figure out yourself. As in other situations, write down the answers to those questions and repeat back what you've heard to check for understanding. This is not only a great learning tool, but it also shows respect for your boss or coworker.

Your energy and upbeat attitude should earn you a great reputation at work. That doesn't mean there won't be conflicts. What counts is how you handle these problems. If a coworker takes a break every five minutes and expects you to pick up the slack, ask to speak to that person away from other staff. No matter how upset you're feeling, don't bark "You don't do your job, so I get stuck doing it for you!" Instead, try a comment like "I feel stressed when I have to take on extra work. How can we support each other so that we both feel like we're doing our fair share?" It could be that your coworker is unwilling to acknowledge that he or she has added to your workload. In a case where these denials continue, you may need to get your supervisor involved.

Customer Service

Whether you work at a clothing store, restaurant, theme park, or hotel, the way you treat customers affects the success of a business. These service industries depend on consumer loyalty, and only customers who are satisfied will keep coming back. When you work in this type of environment, being friendly and upbeat is key. Customers don't care if you had a spat with your mother or your car wouldn't start. They want you to smile, maintain a comfortable level of eye contact, and ask how they are doing. Let them know that you are willing to help with any concern, large or small. That doesn't mean you have to tail them around the boutique or stop by their table every five seconds. Set that positive tone early, check in occasionally, and always focus on their needs.

Look at any problem that does arise as an opportunity. If someone returns a pair of pants with a broken zipper, don't roll your eyes because you think he or she bought too small a size. Take back the merchandise, help the customer find the perfect replacement, and thank him or her for choosing your store. Odds are the customer won't remember the return as much as your willingness to be accommodating. Should the person become truly abusive toward you, seek the help of a supervisor. Pay attention to how your boss handles the situation so that you can learn how to diffuse even the most heated conflicts.

Dealing with the Boss

Whether your work atmosphere is high stress or low-key, your boss is an authority figure and should be treated as such. That doesn't mean he or she can't be approached if you have a question or concern. Just be flexible about timing except in an emergency situation. It's also important to keep what's troubling you in perspective. That slacker coworker may get under your skin, but your boss has many fires to put out every day, so try to see things from his or her point of view. If you're considerate about your boss's many duties, he or she is more likely to hear you out when you do get a chance to meet. Although your concerns may be perfectly legitimate, you want to be seen as a problem solver, rather than a problem creator.

When you're being evaluated on your job performance, listen to everything your boss has to say before responding. Should you disagree with something, focus on facts, rather than emotions. This

When your boss is giving you a job evaluation, listen to his or her feedback before responding.

can be difficult if you feel as if your talents are being minimized or picked apart. Learning to take constructive criticism is part of being a professional, however. While you have every right to be treated fairly, don't get into a blame game or make up excuses. Concentrate on the future and how you can improve going forward.

As in all communication, be honest and direct with your supervisor. When asking for a raise, be clear about your accomplishments. You may even want to bring a list of bullet points to read from should you get nervous. Successful negotiations leave both parties feeling as if they've won, so make sure your boss is bowled over by all you've contributed at work. If it's a day off you need, ask for it instead of just not coming in to work. You earn respect by showing respect, and leaving others in the lurch will do nothing to enhance your professional reputation.

THE RIGHT WORDS TO USE IN ELECTRONIC COMMUNICATION

For most teenagers, it's second nature to communicate electronically. According to the Pew Research Center's Internet & American Life Project, 93 percent of teens from ages twelve to seventeen are online, while 75 percent own a cell phone, and 66 percent send text messages. Moreover, a study by the Nielsen Company found that teens sent an average of 1,742 texts each month! With so many texts zipping back and forth, it might be easy to forget that each one is an exchange of feelings and ideas between two—or more—people. Although there's no denying the convenience of

Caution is required when sending an e-mail or posting on Facebook, since your potential audience is large.

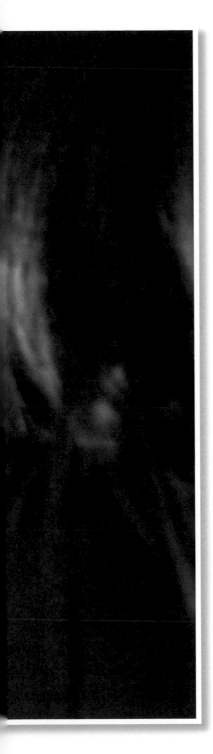

smartphones and tablet computers, there's also a need for caution when communicating electronically.

The news is full of stories of famous people whose e-mails, texts, or tweets have come back to haunt them. These types of communication can even be admissible in a court of law. When you send out an e-mail or post something on Facebook, your potential audience is far greater than in a face-to-face conversation. Although the person you talk with might discuss the conversation with a friend, that's not the same as forwarding your e-mail to thirty other people. Yet people tend to treat electronic communication casually, almost like a sport or video game. But if you're not careful, that LOL could turn into LOT: lots of trouble.

Know Your Audience

As with any communication, it's important to think about what you want to say before you call or hit that "send" button. If you're e-mailing a teacher to clarify an assignment or a potential boss after an interview, be professional. Write in full sentences and avoid using abbreviations or emoticons because they could come across as being disrespectful in this circumstance.

Be professional when sending an e-mail to a teacher or boss. Avoid abbreviations, emoticons, or anything else that might appear disrespectful.

Use caution with friends, too. When you send a message in all caps or with ten exclamation points at the end, it might not be interpreted the way you intended. Remember, the person you're communicating with doesn't have your body language or

tone of voice to help him or her figure out your meaning. For this reason, it's doubly important to choose your words wisely.

On the phone, your tone of voice has added significance. A simple comment like "Yeah, sure" could come across as mocking, rather than enthusiastic, depending on how you say it. All the other person has to go by is your voice, so make sure it matches your meaning. You don't have to rehearse every word you plan to say before dialing. Just be aware of this fact, and as always, try to maintain a positive attitude. If you have a true conflict with someone, it might be best to meet in person. This personal presence avoids the misunderstandings that can occur when relying solely on electronic communication.

Cyberbullying

Along with the rise in the use of social media has come an increase in cyberbullying. According to the Cyberbullying Research Center, cyberbullying is defined as "willful and repeated harm inflicted through the use of computers, cell phones, and other electronic devices." Whether that's sending a nasty text, threatening someone online, or posting private information or photos, this behavior can be very destructive. The fact that the bully can remain anonymous might make him or her more bold. He or she can reach many people at once, too, which makes the victim feel exposed to the world.

There are things you can do to avoid being abused by a cyberbully. Make sure you have strong privacy settings in place and limit the number of "friends" you have on social media sites. Learn how to block calls on your cell phone and don't loan the phone to anyone you don't know well. If you get a cruel or threatening e-mail or text, don't delete it. If the attacks continue, you may need to get your Internet provider or the police involved, so you need that evidence.

Although the urge might be to respond to cyberbullying, that is not the right move. You don't want to get into a war of words with someone who's clearly willing to strike back. It's best to tell your parents or another adult what's happened. Since you've done nothing wrong, there's no need to be embarrassed. Your safety and peace of mind are what matters most.

Community involvement is a vital part of keeping the Internet a safe place for everyone. Teens can contact their representatives in Congress to ask how they can actively support the passage of Internet safety legislation.

Privacy Please

The term "netiquette" refers to the proper manners to use when communicating online. Netiquette involves behavior such as telling the truth about yourself when posting on social networking sites, never "flaming" (insulting) someone, and avoiding e-mail addresses that make you look silly and immature. As Mary Madden of Pew's Internet & American Life Project states, "Social networking requires vigilance, not only in what you post, but what friends post about you." The good news is that young people seem to be getting this message. A study by Pew found that people between the ages of eighteen and twenty-nine were better at monitoring their privacy settings than older adults were. They also deleted comments and took their names off photos more often. This level of care is needed to protect your reputation not only with friends but also within the larger community.

It's vital to know when *not* to communicate online as well. That familiar warning about not talking to strangers also applies to the Internet. Don't pour your heart out to someone in a chat room because you can't know his or her true identity or motives. Never share your Social Security number, address, or other personal information online. Social networking is a fun and efficient way to stay connected, but you can't assume that everyone out there has your best interests in mind.

Communication Control

One of the great things about electronic communication is that you can always be in touch with people. There's a downside to

Although you might be tempted to respond right away to a text that upsets you, it's best to take a minute to collect your thoughts before replying.

that, however. If you're chatting with someone or receive a text, the impulse is to get back to him or her immediately. There are times, though, when it's best to take a break and walk away from your device before responding.

Suppose your friend sends a text that angers you. Since you're not face-to-face, it may seem easier to speak your mind when you respond. But you should never treat your phone (or any device) like a shield you can hide behind. Unless you're planning to move to another continent as soon as you've replied, you will have to see that friend again. Starting an angry back-and-forth via text will only escalate the situation.

To deal with your anger, use deep breathing exercises and calming statements such as "I am in charge of my emotions" to get back on track. Then if you still feel unable to respond in a positive way, set up a time and place to meet. Don't be baited into explaining what's bothering you, either. A simple "Let's talk when we get together" is enough.

Whatever the means of delivery, effective communication should bring people together in a way that enriches everyone involved. Each time you open your mouth—or cell phone or laptop—think of the impact that your words will have on those around you. If you remain upbeat and responsive to the views of others, you will reap the benefits in all aspects of your life.

GLOSSARY

ACCOMMODATING Willing to help.

ACKNOWLEDGE To admit something is real or true.

ARGUMENT A disagreement between two people.

COMMITMENT A pledge or promise.

COMPASSION Sympathy.

COMPROMISE Using communication to find an agreement between people who are in conflict.

CONFIDENCE A feeling of self-assurance.

CONFRONTATIONAL Eager to get into a conflict with someone.

CONSCIENCE An inner sense of what is the right or wrong way to behave.

EFFECTIVE Producing the desired result.

ENCOUNTER To be in contact with.

ENVIRONMENT Surroundings or conditions.

EXPERTISE Skill or knowledge.

FRETTING Worrying.

FRUSTRATING Disappointing or discouraging.

IMMATURE Childish or emotionally underdeveloped; juvenile.

IMPACT To have an effect on.

IMPULSIVE Acting without thinking.

INTERPERSONAL Having to do with personal relationships.

LEGITIMATE Reasonable; able to be defended with logic or justification.

MENTOR A wise or trusted teacher or counselor who guides another person, often someone younger.

MERCHANDISE Products.

NONVERBAL COMMUNICATION Communication through conscious or subconscious hand gestures, facial expressions, and other body movements; also called body language.

OBSESSING Constantly thinking about something or someone.

PERSONNEL A group of people employed in an organization or place of work.

POTENTIAL Capable of becoming or developing into something in the future.

PRIORITY A thing that is regarded as being highest in rank or importance.

REITERATE To say something again or numerous times, usually for emphasis or clarity.

REPUTATION How one is viewed by others.

SELFISH Thinking only of oneself.

SIGNIFICANCE Importance.

SOCIAL NETWORKING Building relationships among people with similar interests through electronic means.

SUPERVISOR A person who manages others in a workplace.

TREMENDOUS Very large in amount, scale, or intensity.

VENT To relieve strong, bad, or hurtful feelings by giving expression to them.

American Psychological Association
750 First Street NE
Washington, DC 20002
(800) 374-2721
Web site: http://www.apa.org
The American Psychological Association provides resources to deal
      with stress, depression, bullying, and workplace issues.

Canadian Safe School Network
11 Peter Street, Suite 608
Toronto, ON M5V 2H1
Canada
(877) 337-0336
Web site: http://www.canadiansafeschoolnetwork.com
This Canadian organization provides resources for students, parents,
      and teachers dealing with bullying and other forms of school
      violence.

Junior Achievement
One Education Way
Colorado Springs, CO 80906
(719) 540-8000
Web site: http://www.ja.org
Junior Achievement offers information on careers, colleges, entrepre-
      neurship, and financial literacy.

National Crime Prevention Council
2001 Jefferson Davis Highway
Suite 901
Arlington, VA 22202
(202) 466-6272
Web site: http://www.ncpc.org

The council's mission is to keep families and communities safe. It offers information on bullying and Internet safety, among other topics.

Society for Safe and Caring Schools and Communities
Barnett House
#504 11010 142 Street
Edmonton, AB T5N 2R1
Canada
(800) 232-7208
Web site: http://www.sacsc.ca
This Canadian organization works to prevent bullying and other forms of harassment through character education and a focus on peaceful conflict resolution.

Youth Canada
140 Promenade du Portage, Phase IV, 4D392
Mail Drop 403
Attn: Youth Operations Directorate
Gatineau, QC K1A OJ9
Canada
(800) 622-6232
Web site: http://www.youth.gc.ca
Youth Canada focuses on issues such as education, job training, and employment.

Youth at Work
U.S. Equal Employment Opportunity Commission
131 M Street NE
Washington, DC 20507

(800) 669-4000

Web site: http://www.eeoc.gov/youth

Part of the Equal Employment Opportunity Commission, Youth at Work teaches young people their rights and responsibilities as employees.

Web Sites

Due to the changing nature of Internet links, Rosen Publishing has developed an online list of Web sites related to the subject of this book. This site is updated regularly. Please use this link to access the list:

http://www.rosenlinks.com/cwc/word

FOR FURTHER READING

Alexie, Sherman. *The Absolutely True Diary of a Part-Time Indian*. New York, NY: Little, Brown, 2009.

Burningham, Sarah O'Leary. *How to Raise Your Parents: A Teen Girl's Survival Guide*. San Francisco, CA: Chronicle Books, 2008.

Carlson, Dale. *Talk: Teen Art of Communication*. Madison, CT: Bick Publishing, 2006.

Chopra, Deepak. *Teens Ask Deepak: All the Right Questions*. New York, NY: Simon & Schuster, 2006.

Cohn, Rachel, and David Levithan. *Nick and Norah's Infinite Playlist*. New York, NY: Knopf, 2008.

Covey, S. *The 7 Habits of Highly Effective Teens*. New York, NY: Fireside, 1998.

Ellsberg, Michael. *The Power of Eye Contact*. New York, NY: HarperPaperbacks, 2010.

Flynn, Sarah Wasser, ed. *Girls' Life Guide to Being the Most Amazing You*. New York, NY: Scholastic, 2010.

Lohmann, Raychelle Cassada. *The Anger Workbook for Teens: Activities to Help You Deal with Anger and Frustration*. Oakland, CA: Instant Help Books, 2009.

Pixley, Marcella. *Freak*. New York, NY: Farrar, Straus and Giroux, 2007.

Senning, Cindy Post, Peggy Post, and Sharon Watts. *Teen Manners: From Malls to Meals to Messaging and Beyond*. New York, NY: Harper Teen, 2007.

Shah, Monica, Mariam MacGregor, and Alison Hill. *Amaze! The Twists and Turns of Getting Along*. New York, NY: Girls Scouts of the USA, 2008.

Shipp, Josh. *The Teen's Guide to World Domination: Advice on Life, Liberty, and the Pursuit of Awesomeness*. New York, NY: St. Martin's, 2010.

BIBLIOGRAPHY

Boy Scouts of America. *Communication* (Merit Badge Series). Irving, TX: Boy Scouts of America, 2010.

Boy Scouts of America. *Family Life* (Merit Badge Series). Rev. ed. Irving, TX: Boy Scouts of America, 2010.

Center for Young Women's Health. "Cyberbullying." Retrieved January 22, 2011 (http://www.youngwomenshealth.org/cyberbullying.html).

Coloroso, Barbara. *The Bully, the Bullied, and the Bystander: From Preschool to High School—How Parents and Teachers Can Help Break the Cycle*. New York, NY: Harper, 2009.

Cyberbullying Research Center. "Definition of Cyberbullying." Retrieved January 5, 2011 (http://www.cyberbullying.us).

Drew, Naomi. *The Kids' Guide to Working Out Conflicts*. Minneapolis, MN: Free Spirit, 2004.

Faber, Adele, and Elaine Mazlish. *How to Talk So Teens Will Listen and Listen So Teens Will Talk*. New York, NY: HarperCollins, 2010.

Holson, Laura M. "Tell-All Generation Learns to Keep Things Offline." *New York Times*, May 9, 2010. Retrieved January 21, 2011 (http:/www.nytimes.com/2010/05/09/fashion/09privacy.html).

Lohman, Raychelle Cassada. "Cyber Etiquette for Teens." *Psychology Today*, 2010. Retrieved December 25, 2010 (http://www.psychologytoday.com/blog/teen-angst/201012/cyber-etiquette-teens).

Lynch, Amy. *A Smart Girl's Guide to Understanding Her Family*. Rev ed. New York, NY: American Girl, 2009.

Nemours Foundation. "Getting Along with Your Teachers." 2008. Retrieved January 5, 2011 (http://kidshealth.org/teen/school_jobs/school/teacher_relationships.html#cat20179).

Nemours Foundation. "School Counselors." 2008. Retrieved January 5, 2011 (http://kidshealth.org/teen/school_jobs/school/school_counselors.html#cat20179).

Nemours Foundation. "Talking to Your Parents or Other Adults." 2009. Retrieved January 3, 2011 (http://kidshealth.org/teen/your_mind/Parents/talk_to_parents.html#cat2059).

Nielsen Company. "In U.S., SMS Text Messaging Tops Mobile Phone Calling." 2008. Retrieved January 22, 2011 (http://www.blog.nielsen.com/nielsonwire/online_mobile/in-us-text-messaging-tops-mobile-phone-calling).

Packer, Alex J. *The How Rude! Handbook of Family Manners for Teens. Avoiding Strife in Family Life*. Minneapolis, MN: Free Spirit, 2004.

Packer, Alex J. *The How Rude! Handbook of School Manners for Teens. Civility in the Hallowed Halls*. Minneapolis, MN: Free Spirit, 2004.

Patterson, Kerry, Joseph Grenny, Ron McMillan, and Al Switzler. *Crucial Conversations: Tools for Talking When Stakes Are High*. New York, NY: McGraw-Hill, 2002.

Shipp, Josh. *The Teen's Guide to World Domination: Advice on Life, Liberty, and the Pursuit of Awesomeness*. New York, NY: St. Martin's, 2010.

Williams, Redford, and Virginia Williams. *In Control: No More Snapping at Your Family, Sulking at Work, Steaming in the Grocery Line, Seething at Meetings, Stuffing Your Frustration*. Emmaus, PA: Rodale, 2006.

Wilson, Zachary. "Pew Survey: Teens Love Facebook, Hate Blogging, Are Always Online, and Don't Use Twitter." FastCompany.com, 2010. Retrieved January 21, 2011 (http://www.fastcompany.com/blog/zachary-wilson/and-how/pew-survey-finds-increase-social-media-internet-time-decrease-blogging-te).

A

allowances, 33
anger, dealing with, 16, 22, 39, 68
anti-bullying policies, 23
apologizing, 11, 23, 38
audience, knowing your, 61–63
auditions, 23

B

blaming, 35, 40, 50, 58
body language, 11, 12, 19, 22, 35, 38, 46, 52, 63
bosses, talking with, 4, 40, 54, 55, 56–58
breathing techniques, 46, 68
bullying, 6, 17, 21, 23–28, 64–65

C

cell phones, 59, 64, 68
chat rooms, 66
clubs, 40
coaches, talking with, 7, 12–14, 40
codes of conduct, 21
communication
    classmates, 17–28
    electronic forms, 4, 59–68
    family life, 4, 26, 30–39, 40, 43, 64
    myths and facts, 29
    nonverbal, 11, 12, 19, 22, 35, 38, 46, 52, 63
    overview, 4–6
    social life, 4, 40, 41–50
    teachers, coaches, and counselors, 4, 7–16, 23, 28, 40, 44
    workplace, 4, 51–58
confidentiality agreements, 16
conflict, dealing with, 4, 15–16, 29, 31, 35–37, 43–44, 54, 55, 63
counselors, talking with, 7, 14–16, 23, 28, 40, 44
criticism, 10, 12, 36, 56, 58
curfews, 31, 35
customer service, 55
cyberbullying, 25, 64–65
Cyberbullying Research Center, 64

D

dating, 43, 44, 45–46, 47, 48
deep breathing techniques, 46, 68
divorce, 40
Drew, Naomi, 22
drinking, 49

E

e-mails, 47, 54, 61–62, 64, 66
emoticons, 62
eye contact, 11, 25, 38, 52, 55

F

Facebook, 47, 61
family meetings, 35–37
flaming, 66
follow-up letters, 54
friends, talking with, 4, 40, 43–44, 48

G

guidance counselor, 10 great
    questions to ask a, 40

I

ice, breaking the, 40
I-messages, 10–12, 23, 46
inner voice, listening to, 48
Internet & American Life Project,
    59, 66
interviews, 52–54, 62

K

Kid's Guide to Working Out Conflicts,
    The, 22

L

language, racially insensitive, 40
laptops, 68
letter writing, 54
listening skills, 6, 16, 31, 38, 39,
    43, 44, 48

M

Madden, Mary, 66
mediators, 16
mentors, 5, 12

N

name-calling, 36–37, 38
netiquette, 66

Nielsen Company, 59
nonverbal communication, 11, 12,
    19, 22, 35, 38, 46, 52, 63
note taking, 36

P

parents, talking with, 26, 30, 31,
    33–35, 40, 64
parties, 40, 49–50
peer pressure, 14, 48–50
Pew Research Center, 59, 66
privacy settings, 64, 66

R

racially insensitive language, 40
raise, asking for a, 58
rejection, 46
relationship, ending a, 47
reputations, 54, 58, 66

S

sarcasm, 21
self-esteem, 46
sexual orientation, 24
Shipp, Josh, 17, 19
siblings, talking with, 30, 31,
    32–33, 38–39, 40
silent treatment, 24
smartphones, 61
smoking, 49, 50
social networking, 40, 47, 61, 64,
    66
stress, 14, 38, 43, 54, 56

T

tablet computers, 61
teachers, talking with, 4, 7, 8–10, 23, 40
teasing, 17, 21, 23, 46
Teen's Guide to World Domination, The, 17, 19
text messages, 44, 47, 54, 59, 61, 64, 68
tone of voice, 6, 12, 21, 23, 25, 28, 35, 38, 46, 54, 63
tweets, 61

U

U.S. Health Resources and Services Administration, 23

V

voice, tone of, 6, 12, 21, 23, 25, 28, 35, 38, 46, 54, 63

W

"word math," 19

About the Author

Jennifer Landau received her MA in creative writing from New York University and her MST in general and special education from Fordham University. An experienced editor, she has also published both fiction and nonfiction. In addition to her work as a special education teacher, Landau has taught writing to high school students and senior citizens. She has a particular interest in expanding inclusion opportunities for special education students and teaching these students self-advocacy skills. When she is not writing, she enjoys reading many different genres of literature and spending time outdoors with her son.

Photo Credits

Cover, back cover, interior graphics Shutterstock.com; pp. 5, 20–21 Hemera Technologies/AbleStock/Thinkstock.com; pp. 8–9 © www.istockphoto.com/ Catherine Yeulet; p. 13 Hill Street Studios/Blend Images/Thinkstock.com; pp. 14–15 Chris Walker/Chicago Tribune/MCT via Getty Images; p.18 Taxi/ Getty Images; pp. 24–25 Jupiterimages/liquidlibrary/Getty Images; pp. 26–27 © www.istockphoto.com/Patrick Herrera; pp. 32–33 Tony Latham/Stone/ Getty Images; pp. 34–35 Ryan McVay/Photodisc/Thinkstock.com; pp. 36–37 © Catchlight Visual Services/Alamy; pp. 42–43 © www.istockphoto.com/ ericsphotography; pp. 44–45 Brand X Pictures/Thinkstock.com; pp. 48–49 Jamie Grill/Iconica/Getty Images; pp. 52–53 © David Young—Wolff/PhotoEdit; pp. 56–57 © Michael Newman/PhotoEdit pp. 60–61 © Earl Clendennen/ Alamy; pp. 62–63 © www.istockphoto.com/Lisa F. Young; pp. 64–65 Roger L. Wollenberg/UPI /Landov; p. 67 © www.istockphoto.com/Ernesto Diaz.

Designer: Nicole Russo; Editor: Kathy Kuhtz Campbell;
Photo Researcher: Amy Feinberg